To :—

Stuart.

with love   22nd December 1961.

Margaret.

CONTENTS

ILLUSTRATIONS IN COLOUR

PUBLISHER'S NOTE

There is a great demand for a clear and concise book of this sort, which provides the basic information necessary for easy identification of some of the more interesting birds of this country.

The brief description of each bird is a supplement to the illustration rather than a guide in itself: it gives colour, shape and size. Under the title " Field Marks " are noted special habits and characteristics. The facts given have been specially chosen to aid recognition, and the silhouettes of the birds drawn to scale within each section.

BIRDS OF FIELD AND WOODLAND

NUTHATCH

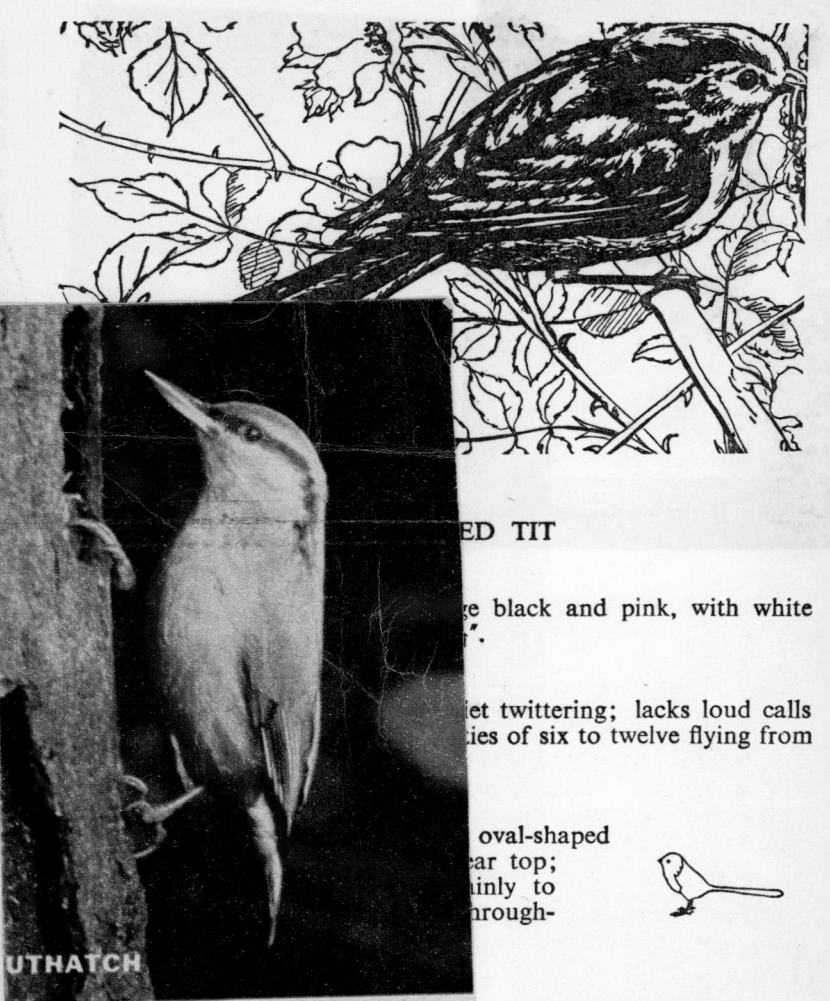

ED TIT

e black and pink, with white
".

et twittering; lacks loud calls
ies of six to twelve flying from

oval-shaped
ar top;
inly to
hrough-

UTHATCH

ow it by its blue-grey back, short tail and long
arp beak. **Expect it** briefly any time. **Feed it**
ts, sunflower seed and fat.

GREAT TIT

Description Head, throat, and middle of underparts black; rest of underparts yellow; white cheeks. Length 6″.

Field Marks Call note resembles saw-sharpening, or " teacher, teacher ". Has many other calls, most of which are louder versions of those made by other tits. Often feeds on the ground.

Nest and Distribution Nest: hole in tree or wall. Is found in woods, gardens, commons and hedgerows, often in suburbs. Scarce in N. Scotland.

BLUE TIT

...ight blue crown, light blue wings
...derparts; yellowish-green
...through eye; white

...nall woodland bird which appears pre-
... cheerful and scolding " tsee tsee tsit ".
...s and hangs from branches upside down

...t: as Great Tit. Common in city parks
... e country. Resident, generally distributed.

BLUE TIT

BLUE

telligent, agil
o introduction
onfined to his
ilk-bottle sea
maller size pr
ests are buil
even lette
hite with sn
e is a valuab
any unwan

COAL TIT

Description Black crown and throat, with white patch at nape of neck and on cheeks, and double white wing-bar. Buff-coloured underparts. Length 4½″.

Field Marks Voice similar to other tits. Likes to creep up tree-trunks.

Nest and Distribution Nests in a hole on or near the ground or in wall or tree stump; common in conifer trees. Less often seen than other tits in built-up areas.

MARSH TIT

Description Brownish, with black crown and chin; paler cheeks and underparts. Length 4½″.

Field Marks Notes as other tits; also " pit-y-chou " and " ship ship ship ".

Nest and Distribution Nest: hole in tree. Has no special preference for marsh country. Not often found in suburban areas. Resident, not found in Scotland, and very local in W. England.

BULLFINCH

Description   Male has bright pink cheeks and underparts.   Head and chin black, large black bill.   Upperparts light grey.   Female and young similar but much duller.   Length 6″.

Field Marks   Soft piping call or penetrating low whistle, often heard when bird is not visible.   White rump conspicuous in flight.

Nest and Distribution   Nests in thick cover such as yew or holly.   A markedly woodland bird, but visits orchards in spring to feed on fruit buds.   Resident, generally distributed.

GOLDFINCH

Description   Forehead, throat and cheeks crimson and white.   Has brilliant yellow patch on black wings.   Legs and stout bill pale flesh-colour. Length 5″.

Field Marks   Continuous liquid " twit " call from perch or on wing. Bounding flight, when white rump is conspicuous; usually seen in flocks.   Hopping gait.

Nest and Distribution   Nests in large gardens, orchards or hedgerows. Often found among thistles or other plants, and in alder trees. Resident but localized.

CHAFFINCH

CHAFFINCH

Description Male: slate-blue head and nape, chestnut back, pink underparts. Hen and young: mostly yellowish-brown and grey. All have white on shoulder, wing-bar, and tail. Length 6″.

Field Marks Call note: " pink, pink ". Has cheerful, rattling song delivered from perch. Very gregarious. White patches are conspicuous in flight.

Nest and Distribution Breeds among trees and hedgerows in gardens, parks, suburbs and countryside. Resident, generally distributed.

HAWFINCH

Description Very large, stout bill. General brownish colour, white on wing and tail conspicuous in flight. Length 7″

Field Marks Easily recognized by stumpy form, with large head, short tail, and shrill call note, " tick ", uttered in flight. Also detected by presence of split stones or empty pea-pods on ground.

Nest and Distribution Nests in orchards, gardens, woods. Resident, but rare in W. and in N. Scotland.

SWAL

Description Upperparts blue-blac
throat chestnut-red; rest of under
white; wings blackish-brown; for

Field Marks Constantly on the win
on telegraph wires and buildings, s

Nest and Distribution Nest: sauce
at the top, usually *inside* building
especially on migration and wher
visitor, uncommon in N.W. Scotlar

SWALLOW

HOUSE MARTIN

Description Upperparts blue-black; rump and underparts white. Forked tail. Length $4\frac{3}{4}''$.

Field Marks White rump and underparts are outstanding features. Same gliding flight as swallow. Gentle twittering song delivered on wing or from perch.

Nest and Distribution

Very gregarious: mud nests are found *outside* buildings, in colonies under eaves, or on face of cliff; have narrow opening at top, otherwise totally enclosed. Summer visitor, local in Ireland.

GREENFINCH

Description   General colour olive-green, with yellow rump and patches on wings and tail. Stout, flesh-coloured bill. Length 6″.

Field Marks Yellow on wings and tail, and forked tail, conspicuous in flight. Twittering song is delivered from top of bush or tree, or in flight.

Nest and Distribution Breeds in hedgerows and bushes. Flocks on stubbles and waste ground, and along sea walls. Resident throughout most of British Isles.

SKYLARK

SKYLARK

Description Brown, streaked darker; underparts paler. White feathers in tail, and white marks over eye. Sometimes shows its crest. Length 7½″.

Field Marks Sustained warbling song, usually delivered when ascending or descending, almost vertically. Also when hovering, often out of sight. Walks, rather than hops, on the ground.

Nest and Distribution Nests in the grass or in growing crops. Prefers open, treeless country, marshy ground, moors, cultivated land. Many emigrate in winter.

WOODLARK

Description Conspicuous buffish stripe from eye to nape. General brown appearance, patterned darker, with buffish, streaked underparts. The tail is short and white-tipped, with greyish outer feathers. Length 6".

Field Marks Mellow, musical song delivered in flight, circling over wide area; usually from trees; sometimes at night. Feeds on ground. Undulating, jerky flight. Often found in family parties.

Nest and Distribution Nests in shelter of grassy tussock. Prefers open country with scattered trees and bushes. Resident; local in England and Wales; uncommon elsewhere.

23

TREE PIPIT

Description Brownish upperparts, streaked darker; paler beneath. Outer tail-feathers white. Legs, flesh pink. Length 6″.

Field Marks Sings while descending from air to perch, ending with " see-ar, see-ar " sound.

Nest and Distribution Nests in depression in the ground. Favours open-wooded districts; likes telegraph poles, which act as song posts. Migrates in winter. Not found in W. Cornwall or N. Scotland.

CUCKOO

Description Grey upperparts, barred underneath with brown. Young has white patch on nape of neck, is often reddish-brown, and barred all over (as in picture). Long, white-spotted tail. Length 14″.

Field Marks Well-known " cooc-coo " note. Female has loud, water-bubbling cry, young has penetrating hiss. Laboured flight; is often surrounded by smaller birds. Long tail and pointed wings are easily recognized.

Nest and Distribution Lays single egg in nest of smaller bird, such as Meadow Pipit. Generally distributed summer visitor.

Opposite: Pipit feeding young cuckoo

BLACKBIRD

BLACKBIRD

Description Male is all black, with orange-yellow bill. Female and young are brownish with spotted throat, not to be confused with the Song Thrush, which is lighter with more distinct spots. Length 10″.

Field Marks Mellow, flutey song, often delivered from tree or chimney stack. General shape, with long tail, which it elevates on alighting, is characteristic. Often stands with head on one side, listening for worms.

Nest and Distribution Nests in hedgerows, bushes, in gardens, parks, and woods. Resident, generally distributed.

26

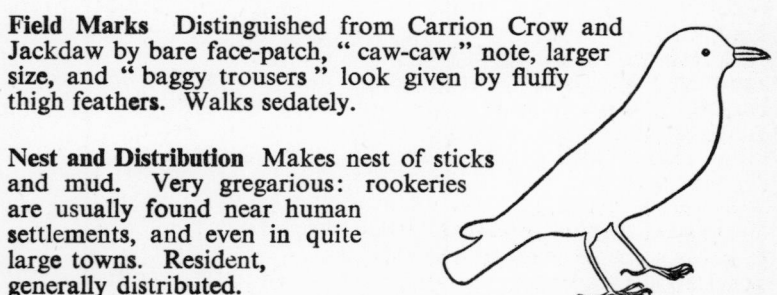

ROOK

ROOK

Description The only all-black bird with a bare patch on its face, at base of thick, blackish bill. Length 18–20″.

Field Marks Distinguished from Carrion Crow and Jackdaw by bare face-patch, " caw-caw " note, larger size, and " baggy trousers " look given by fluffy thigh feathers. Walks sedately.

Nest and Distribution Makes nest of sticks and mud. Very gregarious: rookeries are usually found near human settlements, and even in quite large towns. Resident, generally distributed.

27

CARRION CROW

Description All black, plumage has a greenish glow. Thick black bill, black legs. Length 18–19″.

Field Marks Walks and sidles with ungainly hops. Usually seen in pairs or singly, though sometimes in flocks.

Nest and Distribution Nest: as Rook's, but solitary, not colonial. Common in England and Wales, S. and E. Scotland; not in Ireland.

GOLDCREST

Description Yellowish-green with paler underparts. Dark mark and white bars on wing. Bright orange or yellow crest bordered with black. Smallest European bird. Length 3½″.

Field Marks Coloured crest, small size, and white wing-bars are characteristic. Often hangs upside down. Found in bushes, hedgerows, and woods in small parties, often with other birds.

Nest and Distribution Nest nearly always found in conifers. Resident, generally distributed. Visits east coasts in autumn.

YELLOW HAMMER

Description Male: bright yellow with chestnut upperparts streaked darker. Female and young much less yellow and more brown. Length 6½″.

Field Marks In the breeding season the male is very conspicuous by his colour. Song characteristic: often described as " little bit of bread and no cheese ". Outer tail-feathers are white and prominent in flight.

Nest and Distribution Nests on or near ground in hedges, bushes, etc. Very gregarious, often found in rick-yards. Resident, generally distributed.

JACKDAW

...cept for grey nape and sides of cheek.

...gait quicker and ...ok. Inquisitive,

...ery gregarious. Is ...villages, cliffs, park ...e in a tree, building ...or cliff, usually in ...al in N. Highlands.

JACKDAW

SPARROW HAWK

Description Male: slate-grey; female: grey-brown. Underparts pale, barred with reddish-brown. Broad, bluntish wings, rather short. Tail long. Hooked bill. Length 12–15″.

Field Marks Characteristic flight habit: quick dash along a hedge-row, up and over to pounce on prey. Rapid, gliding flight just over ground. Soars to great height. Plunges with folded wings on prey.

Nest and Distribution Nests chiefly in conifers, oaks and alders, close to main stem. Rarely found in open country. Resident, generally distributed.

31

JAY

Description Pinkish-brown, with barred blue and black mark on wing. Black and white feathers on crown often form crest. Length 14".

Field Marks White rump and blue wing-patch are very noticeable in flight, which is undulating. Harsh screech: " skaak, skaak ".

Nest and Distribution Inhabits woods and well-timbered country, and is often found on oaks at acorn time. Nests in trees or undergrowth. Resident, but local in Scotland and Ireland.

MAGPIE

Description Strikingly pied: black, with prominent white patches on sides of mantle and belly. Long graduated tail is glossed dark green. Length 18".

Field Marks The only large black-and-white land bird with long tail. Usually first seen flying into hedge or tree. Has a chattering cry.

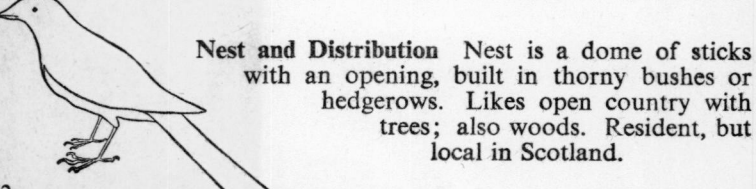

Nest and Distribution Nest is a dome of sticks with an opening, built in thorny bushes or hedgerows. Likes open country with trees; also woods. Resident, but local in Scotland.

KESTREL

KESTREL

Description Commonest British hawk. Chestnut upperparts spotted black; greyish head, rump, and tail, the latter with black band. Underparts buff, streaked with brown. Sharp-pointed wings, long tail. Female duller with brown head and tail, the latter barred. Length 13–14″.

Field Marks Characteristic, habitual hovering, sometimes ending with a drop on to prey. Rapid wing beating and gliding. Sharp scream: " kee-kee-kee ".

Nest and Distribution Lays eggs in hollow on ground, on cliff ledge, in old nests in buildings or trees. Resident, generally distributed.

33

MISTLE THRUSH

Description Greyish-brown, with paler underparts heavily spotted. (Bigger and rounder spots than Song Thrush.) Whitish underwing. Length 11″.

Field Marks Runs and hops on ground with upright carriage. Has characteristic flight, in which wings are closed at regular intervals; white underwing and tail feathers conspicuous. Loud, ringing song, normally delivered from high tree. Alarm note harsh and grating.

Nest and Distribution Usually nests in trees in cultivated country. Very fond of rowan trees in autumn. Resident, generally distributed.

[SO]NG THRUSH

warm olive-brown; underparts much [b]eaks. Flanks yellowish. Length 9″.

[melodi]c song: loud and clear, with notes or [four] times. Usually delivered from high [wit]h head on one side

[nes]t, lined with mud, [trees] and shrubs occur, [commons, woods. [distribut]ed.

35

SONG-THRUSH

GREAT SPOTTED WOODPECKER

Description Black and white, with large white patch on shoulder, and white spots on wing. Under-tail coverts crimson; adult male has red nape. Length 9½″.

Field Marks Flight conspicuously undulating. Climbs up trees. Call is a sharp " tchick "; makes rapid drumming noise on bark of tree, especially on dead wood.

Nest and Distribution Pecks out hole in tree-trunk for nest. Resident. Immigrants seen regularly on east coast in winter.

GREEN WOODPECKER

Description Green, with scarlet crown and " moustache ", and yellow rump conspicuous in flight. Underparts greyish-green. Young are speckled or barred darker. Length 13–14″.

Field Marks Has a far-carrying, laughing call: " pleu-pleu " and " ha-ha ". Undulating flight. Creeps up trees, and hops on ground, where it often feeds.

Nest and Distribution Nest: as Great Spotted Woodpecker, but hole bigger. Likes all well-timbered country, broad-leaved trees rather than conifers. Resident, but local in N. England and very rare in Scotland.

NIGHTINGALE

Description Resembles a large robin in general shape. Upperparts brownish, tail chestnut-brown, underparts paler. Length 6½″.

Field Marks Rarely seen except diving into thick cover. Song, delivered by day as often as by night, is outstandingly rich in volume. There is often a rapid repetition of one note, then slowly repeated " jug jug " sound.

Nest and Distribution Nests on or near ground. Found in thickets, woods, copses, etc. Summer visitor, mainly south and east of line from S. Yorkshire to Devon.

HOUSE-SPARROW

HOUSE SPARROW

Description Upperparts brownish, streaked with black. Crown, nape and rump ashy-grey; chestnut streak on each side of head. Throat and breast black. Length 6″.

Field Marks This is a perky and well-known town bird. Found also in the country near buildings, or in cornfields, rickyards, etc., with other seed-eaters. Hops on ground.

Nest and Distribution Very gregarious; found in large flocks. Resident, generally distributed.

HEDGE SPARROW

Description Upperparts brown, streaked darker. Chin, throat, and breast bluish-grey. Length 5½″.

Field Marks An inconspicuous bird. Hops slowly along ground, with lowered head. Is often betrayed by characteristic call note, "tique, tique", and sweet little warbling song.

Nest and Distribution Nests in hedges, stick heaps, and thick undergrowth. Found in suburbs as well as in the country. Resident, generally distributed.

ROBIN

ROBIN

Description Olive-brown above, with bright orange-red face, throat and breast. Young is brown speckled with buff. Length 5¾″.

Field Marks Shape, and quick perky way of moving, characteristic. Very confiding, and will approach quite close to people.

Nest and Distribution Will nest almost anywhere on or near ground, even in old shoes. A common suburban bird, generally distributed. Not often found in open country away from cover.

40

CORN BUNTING

Description Resembles Sparrow, but larger, and has no white on tail feathers. Sturdy build, with heavy head and bill; otherwise inconspicuous brownish bird, streaked darker. Underparts lighter, less marked. Length 7".

Field Marks Gregarious. Flies in flocks, uttering characteristic flight song. Also has persistent, rather discordant jangling note. Feeds on ground, perches on bushes and telegraph wires. Male often flies with legs dangling.

Nest and Distribution Nests in clumps of grass, thistles. Haunts gorsy commons, cultivated, almost treeless land. Resident, generally distributed.

LAPWING or PEEWIT

Description Dark, metallic green upperparts often look black. Throat black, underparts white, but no black on throat in winter. Prominent crest, long legs. Length 12½″.

Field Marks Flight is unusual, with bent and rounded wings; often gives striking and acrobatic display in which wings make loud throbbing noises. Call note: " pee-wit ". **Runs on ground, and wades in water.**

Nest and Distribution Favours open places such as farmland, damp rushy fields, coastal mudflats and sands. Resident, generally distributed.

WREN

Description Rufous brown, barred darke[r] flanks, and tail. Short tail is nearly always [upright.]

Field Marks Often creeps along the ground li[ke] warbling song, usually delivered from a pe[rch,] for the bird's size.

Nest and Distribution Found almost anyw[here from] sea-level to mountain top, but not in la[rge numbers.] Nest is well hidden, neatly domed, wi[th] entrance at side, may be anywhere. Resid[ent.]

WREN

WOODCOCK

Description Warm brown, streaked and barred darker. Bill is very long. Length 13″.

Field Marks Often rises from close underfoot, flies fast, and twists among trees, carrying bill downwards when flying. Difficult to see on ground because of colouring. Has unusual display flight, called roding, when it utters distinct, croaking call.

Nest and Distribution Is found chiefly in damp oak woods or feeding in marshes or bogs. Resident; prefers west and north, and east coast in winter.

44

SONG THRUSH

Know it by its spotted breast, buff patch under wing. **Expect it** in very cold weather. **Feed it** by scattering scraps on the ground.

SHRIKE

...wn above, creamy below. Crown,
...ail black, outer side of base white.
...emale has brown bars on underparts.

...habit of perching very high on tree or bush
and ...and down or sideways. Flight low and swooping,
pointe...ceable.

Nest and Distribution Nest: in bushes or hedges,
usually of thorn; 5–20 ft. up. Local summer
visitor, chiefly to S. and E. England.

WHEATEAR

Description Male: clear, purplish-grey upperparts; underparts
buffish, rump and base of tail white, contrasting with black tip.
Black line through eye, prominent white stripe above. Female:
upperparts dull brown, underparts buff. Length 6″.

Field Marks Often seen hopping on the ground, and chasing flies.
White rump conspicuous in flitting flight.

Nest and Distribution Nests in hole on ground
or under stones. Frequents open, uncultivated
country, downs, moorlands, sand-dunes. Summer
visitor, local.

45

CHIFF CHAFF

Description Upperparts olive-brown, underparts dull white, tinged with buff and yellow. Legs and bill black. Length 4½″.

Field Marks Restless flitting flight. Characteristic " chiff chaff " or " zip-zip " song, interspersed with small, guttural sound.

Nest and Distribution Domed nest is found in undergrowth, nearly always in wooded areas. Summer visitor, arriving late March. Generally distributed, but local in Scotland.

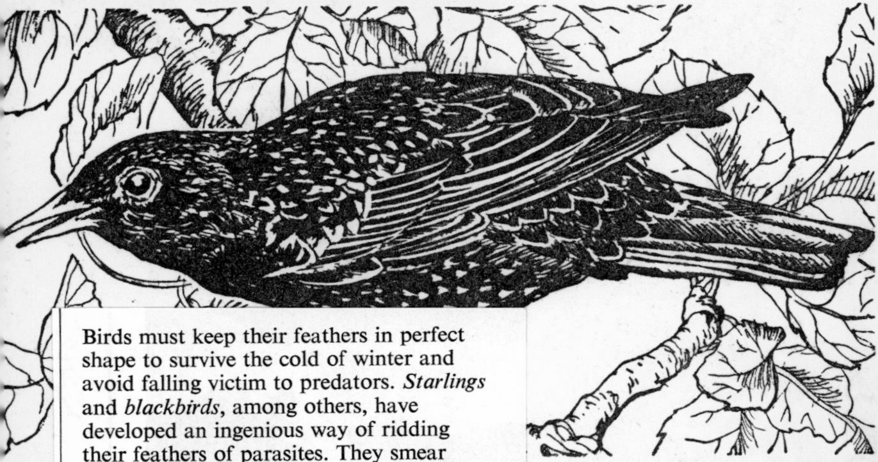

Birds must keep their feathers in perfect shape to survive the cold of winter and avoid falling victim to predators. *Starlings* and *blackbirds*, among others, have developed an ingenious way of ridding their feathers of parasites. They smear themselves with ants, which squirt out formic acid—a highly effective insecticide. The BOOK OF BRITISH BIRDS reveals the lengths to which birds will go to keep their feathers in condition.

D
ti
th

F
S
o
in

STARLING

N
holes in trees, buildings, etc. Resident and
Large numbers arrive on east coast in wi

47

STARLING

FIELDFARE

Description Blue-grey crown, nape, and rump, chestnut back, black tail. Buff underparts spotted darker. Yellow bill. Length 10″.

Field Marks Has unusual flight in which wings are closed for a perceptible amount of time, as with Mistle Thrush. Light underwing, long tail, and grey rump conspicuous. Call note a harsh " trak trak ".

Nest and Distribution Highly gregarious. Nearly always flocks in fields and open country. Eats hedgerow fruits, especially in hard weather. Winter visitor, generally distributed.

LINNET

LINNET

Description Brownish, streaked darker. [...] has crimson forehead and breast; duller i[...] dark-brown bill. Length 5–6″.

Field Marks Bounding or dancing flight, when white wing-bars and margins of tail are conspicuous. Incessant chatter while in flight. Pleasant twittering song, often in chorus.

Nest and Distribution Gregarious at all times, often nesting in colonies, in thickets of gorse, bramble, etc., or hedgerows. Resident; generally distributed, except in Scottish Highlands.

WHITETHROAT

Description Brownish, with rufous wings and white throat. Head and neck greyish. Long tail, with white feathers which are conspicuous in flight. Length 5½″.

Field Marks Characteristic song; a rapid, twittering, rather harsh, warble, usually delivered from perch or in short, vertical flight. Skulks unobtrusively in thick undergrowth, especially nettles.

 **Nest and Distribution** Nests close to the ground in undergrowth and low bushes. Eats berries and soft fruits in gardens. Summer visitor, generally distributed except in N. Scotland.

NIGHTJAR

Description Brownish-grey, mottled darker and paler. Male has white marks on wings and tail; large eyes, small bill. Length 10½″.

Field Marks Inconspicuous on ground or perched *along* branch during day. Seen at nightfall; long tail and pointed, white-marked wings distinctive in flight, which is silent and twisting. Sometimes makes a loud, clapping noise with wings. Call note: " cu-ic ". Song: far-carrying " churr-rr ", at dusk and night-time.

Nest and Distribution Lays two eggs on ground. Found in heaths, woodland clearings. Summer visitor, local.

51

WOOD PIGEON

Description Upperparts greyish-blue; underparts brownish-purple, merging into paler blue-grey. Neck: green and purple, with conspicuous patch of white. Pinkish bill and legs, pale yellow eye. Length 17″.

Field Marks. Well-known note, " kuk-oo-roo, coo-ooo ", ending with abrupt " kuk ". Flight fast and direct, taking off with noisy clatter of wings when disturbed. Very gregarious.

Nest and Distribution Likes wooded country, and town parks. Resident, but uncommon in N. Scotland.

PHEASANT

...ghtly coloured plumage, female is brownish; ... from all other birds by their size and long

...he long, graduated tail is characteristic in ... running. The cry of the male is a harsh ...ften followed by a beating of wings.

...d Distribution Nests in a hollow in the ... Seen in woodlands and on well-timbered commons and heaths. Common throughout British Isles, except Ireland.

PARTRIDGE

Description Brown, with darker and lighter markings. Greyish breast has dark chestnut horseshoe. Legs grey; yellowish in juveniles. Chestnut tail. Length 12½″.

Field Marks Characteristic flight: fast beating of wings, alternating with gliding on down-curved wings. High-pitched, loud, grating call and rapid cackle. Runs very fast.

Nest and Distribution Found in small parties called coveys, in cultivated country. Nests in hedgerows or open field. Resident, generally distributed.

SPOTTED FLYCATCHER

Description Upperparts grey-brown, underparts paler, dark streaks on crown and breast. Length 5½".

Field Marks Constantly darts from perch to catch insect, then darts back to same or nearby place. Song consists of several notes which sound as if uttered by numerous birds engaged in conversation. Alarm note, " tzee ", rather like Robin.

Nest and Distribution Nests against wall or tree trunk. Found in gardens, parks, suburban areas, and woods. Summer visitor, generally distributed.

BLACKCAP

Description Male: crown black. Hen and juveniles: reddish-brown cap. Upperparts greyish-brown, underparts white. Chin and throat ash-grey. Thin black bill. Length 6¼".

Field Marks Characteristic song is high, melodic warble; hard " taac ", delivered from well-concealed perch, is call note.

Nest and Distribution Nests in undergrowth. Frequents woods, shrubs (especially rhododendrons), and places where there is much undergrowth. Summer visitor; fairly well distributed, except in N.E. Scotland.

BARN OWL

Description Upperparts golden buff, mottled with grey. Underparts white, speckled. Facial disc is white, heart-shaped; eyes black; hooked, whitish bill. Rounded wings, feathered legs and feet. Length 13½″.

Field Marks Usually silent, but has a prolonged shriek, also hisses and snores. Flight slow and flapping. Generally hunts late afternoon or night. spends day in hollow tree or hole in building.

Nest and Distribution Nests in cavities as described above. Resident; generally, but not abundantly, distributed.

TAWNY OWL

Description Upperparts vary from rich chestnut-brown to greyish-brown. Underparts buff, streaked with dark brown. Facial disc greyish, eyes black, bill hooked, and pale greenish-yellow. Feathered legs and feet. Length 18–19″.

Field Marks Flight slow and flapping. Familiar call is " hoo-hoo-hoo " and " ke-wick, ke-wick ". Hunts at night, but is sometimes seen by day, mobbed by parties of small birds.

Nest and Distribution Lays eggs in tree holes or in old nests. Resident, generally distributed.

LONG-EARED OWL

Description Buff, mottled darker and lighter; underparts with dark longitudinal streaks. " Ear " tufts distinct. Length 14″.

Field Marks Rarely seen during day, unless at rest close to tree-trunk (often fir or larch); or being mobbed by small birds. Silent flight, familiar long-drawn " ooo-oooo " moan. Preys on mice and other small mammals and birds.

Nest and Distribution Nests in squirrel hole or old nest, occasionally on ground. Always in wooded country. Resident; generally distributed; local in Wales; the only Owl breeding in Ireland.

BIRDS OF HILL, MOOR AND MARSH

GOLDEN EAGLE

Description Chocolate to
tawny-brown, tinges of
golden-yellow on back of
neck. Young darker, with
white tail. Powerful bill,
broad, rounded wings and tail.
Length 30–35″.

Field Marks Wing beats leisurely
and powerful. Glides on motionless wings, soars to great heights.
Swoops on quarry (birds, small
mammals, carrion), lifts it into the
air. Perches, immobile, on crags
and trees for long periods of time.
Usually silent, but has shrill yelp,
and barking call.

Nest and Distribution Nests on cliff ledge, sometimes in trees. Resident in Scottish Highlands and Hebrides, rare elsewhere.

HOODED CROW

Description Stout bill, feathered at base. Grey mantle and underparts, rest of plumage black. Length 18–19″.

Field Marks Note: a hoarse caw. Feeds mainly on ground. Not
found in large flocks. Wing beats slow and regular. Smashes hard
shelled food (nuts and molluscs) by dropping from a height.

Nest and Distribution Nests in trees, bushes, cliff ledges, or on
ground. Prefers fairly open country: cultivated lands, mountains
and coasts. Resident in Ireland,
Isle of Man, and Scottish Highlands;
elsewhere, winter visitor.

MARSH HARRIER

Description Dark, reddish-brown with lighter, yellowish shoulders and head. Long wings, legs and tail. Male has ash-grey tail, and grey on wings. Length 24–25".

Field Marks Flight characteristic: low over reeds or crops, slow wing beats followed by gliding, legs hanging down; at times rises in wide circles, pounces suddenly on prey. Settles on posts, but never far from ground.

Nest and Distribution Nests in reed beds and marsh vegetation. Summer visitor to Norfolk and Suffolk.

HOBBY

472 pages like
open your eye

HOBBY

Description Long, sickle-shaped wings. Upperparts dark, slatey-brown; underparts whitish, with conspicuous black, longitudinal streaks. Rust-red thighs and flanks. Black moustachial stripe. Length 12–14″.

Field Marks Characteristic flight: rapid beats, alternating with long glide on motionless wings. Feeds on the wing, insects and small birds: falls on prey from great height. Cry, a whistling, repetitive " quic-ic ". Prefers open country for hunting.

Nest and Distribution Usually nests in woods or clump of trees, in deserted crow's nest. Favours pine trees. Summer visitor, mostly south of Thames.

CHOUGH

Description Long curved, bright red bill (orange in young), and red legs. Glossy black plumage. Length 15″.

Field Marks Generally seen on sea cliffs, but also hilly districts inland. Has buoyant, acrobatic flight, frequently soaring and gliding, progressing with leisurely flapping. Walks, runs, and hops on ground. Long-drawn " kyaaa " note during which it flicks up tail and wings.

Nest and Distribution Nests in crevices on cliffs or quarries. Resident, but localized: chiefly on west coasts.

CROSSBILL

Description   Male is bright red, with darker wings and tail, the latter deeply forked.   The stout bill has mandibles crossed.   Female and young greenish-yellow, streaked darker, especially underneath.   Length 6″.

Field Marks   Tame, parrot-like bird; hangs upside down on branches, mainly on conifers, and attacks cones.   Sidles along branches; rarely seen on ground except when drinking.   Unmistakable " chup chup " note, usually in flight.

Nest and Distribution   Nests generally in Scots pine.   Resident in central Scotland and E. England.   Periodically large flocks appear in various parts of England, and breed upon occasion.

ROCK DOVE

Description   Distinctive white rump, noticeable in flight.   General colour bluish-grey, with black wing-bars, iridescent greens and reds around the neck.   Compact shape, with rounded breast.   Red eye. Length 13″.

Field Marks   Swift, dashing flight, often low over water.   Rises with noisy clatter of wings, glides.   Seldom perches on trees—usually on rocks, or ground.   Note: " croooo-crooooo ".

Nest and Distribution   Nests in caves or on cliffs.   Resident on sea coasts, chiefly Scotland and Ireland.

SISKIN

Description General colour greenish-yellow, with underparts more yellow, striped in female and young. Wings darker, with white wing-bars. Male is more distinct, with yellow rump, black chin and head. Length 4¼″.

Field Marks Keeps mostly to trees, flitting quickly and restlessly from branch to branch. Often associates with Redpolls: its favourite trees are conifers and alders. Shrill clear call and lively song.

Nest and Distribution Nests high in conifers. Resident, but localized: Ireland, E. and N. Scotland, N. England and N. Wales.

TWITE

Description General colour tawny-brown, streaked darker, with underparts paler. Indistinct white wing mark. Male has pink rump. Bill yellow in winter, otherwise grey. Length 5¼".

Field Marks Feeds on ground, but perches on bushes and trees. Often appears in large flocks. Note: a twanging " chweek " and " tsooek ", and a metallic twitter. Flight rapid and undulating.

Nest and Distribution Nests in colonies on or near ground, in open moorland. In winter, often found on coastal marshes. Resident in N. England, Scotland, Ireland.

REDPOLL

Description Crimson forehead and black chin are unmistakable. Breast and rump of male tinted pink in summer. Upperparts brownish, streaked darker. Buff wing-bars. Length 4½".

Field Marks Characteristic song flight: looping and circling with slow wing beats; song repetitive, rippling trill. Often flocks with Siskin, keeps up continuous, metallic twittering, and maintains acrobatic postures.

Nest and Distribution Nests in high hedges, trees, tall heather. Haunts birches, alders, osier beds, coniferous trees. Resident in most of Scotland and Ireland, N. and E. England, local elsewhere.

REDSTART

Description Distinctive orange tail; black face and throat in male, blue-grey upperparts with white forehead, and orange underparts. Females and young duller, but with tail as adult male. Length 5½".

Field Marks Unmistakable, up-and-down quivering of bright tail. Constantly flits among branches or catches insects in the air. Bobbing movement when on ground, but usually perches on trees. Brief, melodious warble, metallic alarm call.

Nest and Distribution Nests in tree holes, stone walls. Frequents chiefly gnarled woods in hilly country; local in other haunts. Summer visitor, chiefly to N. and W. Britain.

SHORT-EARED OWL

Description General colour tawny, heavily blotched and barred with dark brown and buff. Well-defined facial disc. " Ear " tufts indistinct. Length 15″.

Field Marks Strong, buoyant flight with slow wing beats and glides. Often crouches, well concealed, on ground. Prolonged, mechanically regular " snore " and hoarse croak.

Nest and Distribution Nest is hollow in heathery ground. Frequents moorland country. Resident in Scotland, W. Wales, E. Anglia, Peak and Pennine areas of England.

KITE

Description Deeply forked tail, long, narrow
wings, with distinctive white patch on underside.
... greyish-white.

use of chemicals to destroy insects,
...nts and weeds has revolutionised
...culture. But by destroying these pests
...as also harmed the birds which eat
...n. Small quantities of poison in their
...y have accumulated in the bodies of
...lators such as the *peregrine*, resulting
...nfertility or death. The BOOK OF
...ISH BIRDS shows how birds have
...pted to life in the 20th century, and
... you what man is doing to protect
...n.

... n wide circle,
... es shrill, mewing
... ts, rabbits, frogs,

... of sticks close to main stem of oak.
... ith wooded valleys. Resident; con-

...EGRINE

...INE FALCON

... pperparts in male, brown in female,
... moustachial stripe black. Under-
... black. Long pointed wings, tapering
... 15–19".

... flight: rapid wing beats, then long
... rapidly on prey (often pigeon), wings
... Alarm call:

... d nest, or cliff ledge.
... marshes. Resident;
general in Wales, Scotland, and Ireland, chiefly
coastal cliffs in England.

71

BLACK-THROATED DIVER

Description Head and nape grey, throat black. Black-and-white streaks at side of neck and breast. Upperparts boldly patterned black and white, underparts white. Throat white in winter time. Length 27″.

Field Marks Powerful flight, planes rapidly down to water. Dives effortlessly and swims underwater. Note, a guttural " kwuk-kwuk ".

Nest and Distribution Nests on islets and shores of larger lochs, in hilly country. Resident in N. and W. Scotland; winter visitor to coasts elsewhere.

(Silhouette is similar to that of Red-throated Diver. See frontispiece for illustration in colour)

RED-THROATED DIVER

Description Grey-brown upperparts, with grey head and sides of neck. Chestnut-red patch on throat, white underparts. Bill slightly uptilted. In winter, upperparts are very thickly speckled with white. Length 21″.

Field Marks Can submerge whole body and swim rapidly underwater. Also swims with only head submerged, looking for fish.

Nest and Distribution Breeds on small ponds and lochs, as well as on larger ones. Resident. Breeds Scottish Highlands. Visits other coasts in winter, when throat is white.

(See frontispiece for illustration in colour)

72

GREAT NORTHERN DIVER

Description Largest of the divers. Head and neck black, with incomplete collar of vertical white bars. Upperparts greenish with white transverse markings. Underparts white, with black streaks at side of breast. Duller in winter; throat then white. Length 30–33".

Field Marks Clumsy on land, but dives and swims effortlessly. Takes to the air slowly and ponderously, but flight is powerful and direct. Generally silent.

Nest and Distribution Does not nest in Britain. Rare, but generally distributed on all coasts in winter.

DOTTEREL

Description Broad white eye-stripes, meeting on nape. Brown breast is separated from chestnut lower-breast by white band. Upperparts blackish-brown, cheeks and throat whitish. Tail bordered with white, belly black. Length 9".

Field Marks Tame, inconspicuous bird, difficult to see. Runs quickly on ground. Gregarious. Sweet, twittering whistle: " wit-e-weee ".

Nest and Distribution Nests on the ground. Summer visitor, breeding only on very highest mountains of Lake District and Scotland.

(See following pages for silhouettes and illustration)

73

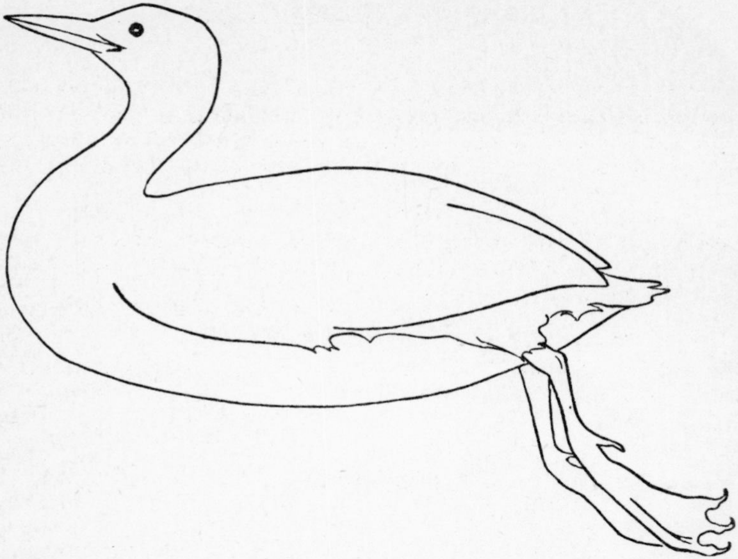

Above: Great Northern Diver

Left: Dotterel

RING OUZEL

Description Resembles Blackbird (see page 26), but male, as well as black plumage, has white crescent on breast, and wings appear greyer than rest of body. Female and young are browner. Female has narrow brown throat patch. Length 9½″.

Field Marks Hops or runs on ground; on alighting, raises tail; puts head on one side, "listening" for worms. Clear piping song, with some harsh chattering.

Nest and Distribution Nests on river banks or in old buildings. Summer visitor to most hilly and mountainous districts, especially Scotland.

CAPERCAILLIE

Description Noticeably large and dark. Male: glossy dark slate-grey, with darker throat and head, blue-green on breast. Tail rounded, feathered legs. Red wattle over eye. Female: mottled lighter, has rufous patch on breast. Length 36″, female 26″.

Field Marks Breaks noisily out of cover, otherwise glides silently on down-curved wings, alternating with quick wing beats. Settles frequently on ground. Song resembles knocking.

Nest and Distribution Nests on ground. Resident in Scotland, in coniferous forests. Became extinct, was reintroduced in eighteenth century.

PTARMIGAN

Description Grouse-like bird, with distinctive plumage: all white in winter, except for black near eye, and white underparts and underwings in summer. Rest of summer plumage is mottled dark brown and grey. Red wattle over eye. Legs feathered. Length 13-14″.

Field Marks White plumage gives pied appearance in summer. Whirring flight, alternating with gliding on down-curved wings. Walks, and crouches low when uneasy. Hoarse croak or snore.

Nest and Distribution Confined to high mountains in Scotland, including islands. Nests on stony ground or in short heather or grass. Resident.

77

BUZZARD

Description Upperparts brown, underparts barred and streaked brown and white. Yellow legs, hooked bill. Sturdy build. Length 20–22″.

Field Marks Characteristic soaring, spiralling flight, with broad, rounded wings almost horizontal, wing-tips spread like fingers, and tail expanded. Direct flight is more laboured. Plaintive mewing. Feeds on rabbits and other small animals, which it catches on ground.

Nest and Distribution Nests on cliffs, trees, or ground. Frequents wild, hilly country, preferably wooded, and rocky coasts.

MERLIN

Description Smallest British hawk. Male's upperparts dark grey, underparts warm beige, streaked with brown; female's, dark brown, underparts buff, streaked with brown. Legs yellow. Length 10–13″.

Field Marks Flies close to ground, captures smaller birds. Chattering scream when near nest: " quik-k-k ". Always found in open country, and marshes in winter.

Nest and Distribution Nests on ground, among heather; or in old nests on sea cliffs or in trees. Resident in Pennines, Wales, moors of N. England, and in Scotland and Ireland.

BLACK GROUSE

Description Lyre-shaped tail (male), and white wing-bar, unmistakable. Female: warm brown, barred with black, forked tail. Male: darker, almost black, with red wattle over eye, white under-tail feathers. Length 22″, female 15″.

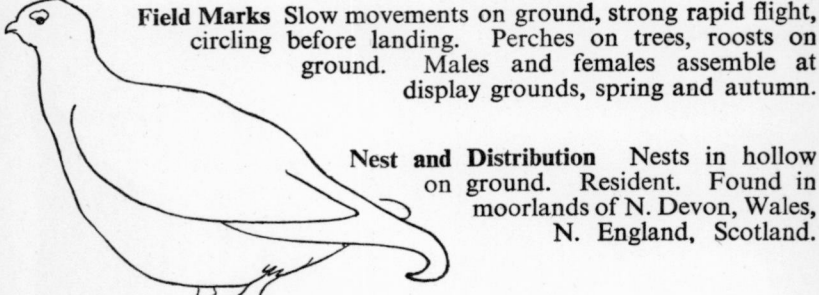

Field Marks Slow movements on ground, strong rapid flight, circling before landing. Perches on trees, roosts on ground. Males and females assemble at display grounds, spring and autumn.

Nest and Distribution Nests in hollow on ground. Resident. Found in moorlands of N. Devon, Wales, N. England, Scotland.

RED GROUSE

Description Dark red-brown, darker in winter than in summer. Whitish, feathered legs, large red wattle over eye. Female lighter than male at all seasons. Length 13–15″.

Field Marks Usually seen rising with whirring wings from heather. Has strong, rapid flight, alternating with gliding on down-curved wings. Note: " go-back, go-back ".

Nest and Distribution Nests on ground in hollow, sheltered by heather or grass. Resident on moors of N. England, Wales, Scotland, and Ireland.

CRESTED TIT

Description Distinguished from other tits by pointed crest. Cheeks and neck whitish, throat and collar black. Black mark through eye curves round ear coverts. Upperparts brownish, with wings and tail darker. Underparts dirty white or buff. Length $4\frac{1}{2}''$.

Field Marks Has characteristic note: a lively, purring trill unlike other tits. Found in small parties, usually in conifers.

Nest and Distribution Nests in pine stumps, in hole or crevice, or in alders and birches. Resident, confined to pine forests of central highlands of Scotland.

WILLOW TIT

Description Black crown and chin, white cheeks. Underparts buff, upperparts brownish, with indistinct white wing-bar. Similar to Marsh Tit, but crown is sooty rather than glossy. Length 4½″.

Field Marks Song erratic, often silent. Characteristic notes harsh " zurr-zurr-zurr " and high-pitched " zi-zi-zi ". Short, direct flight, with rapid, laboured wing beats, as other tits.

Nest and Distribution Makes hole in birch, alder, or willow stump, usually in marshy places, damp woods. Resident, very localized. Unknown in Ireland and N. Scotland.

BEARDED TIT

Description Striking, glossy black moustachial stripe, blue-grey head. General colour tawny-brown, buffish underparts. Long, graduated tail, with white at sides. Wing banded lengthwise with white, brown, black and buff. Female duller; no moustachial stripe, but has black eye-mark. Length 6″.

Field Marks Low, undulating flight. Creeps up reeds and among vegetation. Notes: " ping, ping " and " tic-tic ".

Nest and Distribution Nests low among reeds, in large reed-beds. Resident on broads of E. Anglia.

GREY WAGTAIL

Description   Slate-grey upperparts, long tail, and yellow under-tail coverts distinct from other wagtails. Greenish-yellow rump, underparts buff to yellow. Male has white eye stripe and black throat in spring, female white throat marked with black. Length 7″.

Field Marks   Walks or runs swiftly, constantly moving tail up and down. Undulating flight; perches on boulders. Metallic " tzee ree " note.

and Distribution   Nests in hole on cliff, or on ledge near rocky streams in mountainous districts; lowland ponds, coasts in Resident; widespread near running water; local breeder S. gland.

YELLOW WAGTAIL

mantle, crown, and ear coverts, yellow head tail dark brown, with buff wing-bars and s. Female duller. Length 6½″.

PIED WAGTAIL

ground, sometimes feeds among cattle. Un-" tsweep " note, brief warbling song, during down.

Nest and Distribution   Nests on ground, in crops or grass. Frequents cattle pastures (chiefly lowland), cultivated fields, shingle beaches and sand-dunes. Summer visitor; local in England and Wales; uncommon in Scotland.

ROCK PIPIT

Description Upperparts dark olive-brown, underparts lighter, spotted and streaked darker. Long tail has smoke-grey outer feathers. Dark-brown legs. Length 6¼".

Field Marks Erratic, jerky flight. Perches on rocks or low eminences. Runs quickly on ground. Distinctive song: short phrases, delivered while ascending and planing down.

Nest and Distribution Nests sheltered by vegetation on shore or cliff. Resident; generally distributed: found on any rocky shore, local east and south coasts of England.

WHINCHAT

Description Prominent white stripe (buff in female) above eye. Streaked brown upperparts, darker wings and tail. Underparts warm buff. White at side of base of tail, and white wing patch. Female and young duller. Length 5″.

Field Marks Perches on tops of plants and bushes, flying jerkily from one to another. Bobs on ground, flicking tail and wings. Scolding " tic-tic " note, and warbling song.

Nest and Distribution Nests on ground or in low bushes. Frequents mountain slopes, heaths and grasslands where there are low bushes. Summer visitor. Common locally.

STONECHAT

Description Male has black head, with white at sides of neck, on rump and wing. Upperparts almost black, underparts chestnut. Female and young lighter, more streaked, without white on neck or rump. Length 5″.

Field Marks Perches on tops of plants, flitting tail and wings. Plumper and more upright than Whinchat. Notes: repetitive " tsak tsak " and " hweet chat ".

Nest and Distribution Nests on or near ground at foot of gorse or other low bush. Resident; locally distributed in heathland, moorland and downland country, especially near coast.

SEDGE WARBLER

Description Conspicuous, creamy-white eye stripe. Dark brown, streaked crown and upperparts. Tawny rump conspicuous in flight. Underparts buff or whitish. Graduated tail. Length 5″.

Field Marks Creeps in undergrowth, clinging to reeds and perching on tall plants. Flies low, with tail down, short distances only. Harsh churring song oft-repeated, and includes imitative phrases, some of which are sweet, delivered from exposed perch or in flight, but usually from cover; sometimes at night.

Nest and Distribution Nests in waterside vegetation close to ground. Inhabits reed beds, marshes, ditch banks. Summer visitor, generally distributed.

REED WARBLER

Description Upperparts olive-brown, tinged with rufous especially on rump. Underparts white at throat, shading to buff. Indistinct eye stripe. Slaty-brown legs. Length 5″.

Field Marks Rarely seen away from reeds growing in water, where it restlessly flits and creeps up stems, only flying short distances. Note: a low " churr-churr-churr . . ." song; less varied than Sedge Warbler.

Nest and Distribution Well-built nest has very deep cup, is suspended between reeds or other marsh vegetation. Summer visitor to England south of Humber, and Wales.

GRASSHOPPER WARBLER

Description Olive-brown upperparts, with indistinct dark streaks; buff breast, lightly streaked; long graduated tail. Obscure eye stripe. Length 5″.

Field Marks Shy, secretive bird, but has noticeable, rapid high-pitched trill, with mechanical effect, similar to grasshopper, but louder. Often sings at night. Creeps in undergrowth, seldom flies.

Nest and Distribution Nests in grass clumps. Summer visitor; local; rare in Scotland. Frequents fairly open country: moors, commons, marshes.

PIED FLYCATCHER

Description Male conspicuous in spring; black above, white below, with white forehead and wing-bar. Otherwise olive-brown above, whitish below, with buff wing-bar. Length 5″.

Field Marks Perches on trees, making sallies after insects. Clings to trunk, also feeds on ground, moving tail up and down and flicking wings.

Nest and Distribution Nests in tree holes, buildings. Favours wooded, hilly country, especially near streams. Summer visitor; local: mostly Wales, Scottish border counties, W. England.

CURLEW

Description Long bill curved down; long legs; general brown colour, streaked darker. White rump noticeable in flight. Tail darker. Length 19–25″.

Field Marks Very shy bird. Distinctive " cour lee " note, loud and musical. Probes into sand and wades in water. Commonly in parties, flocks flying in angled formations, swiftly and with strong wing beats. Planes before landing.

Nest and Distribution Nests on ground in boggy moors. Otherwise keeps to mud-flats and estuaries and some shores. Resident; common on all coasts; only local breeder in Midlands, E., and S.E. England; regular elsewhere.

92

REDSHANK

Description Legs and base of long bill, red. White rump, tail coverts, and crescent on wing conspicuous in flight. Mantle grey-brown, head, neck and breast greyish, streaked brown. Length 11″.

Field Marks Often wades in shallow water, has bobbing motion of head and keeps wings raised a moment after landing. Shy and restless. Musical whistling note.

Nest and Distribution Nest well concealed in grass tuft, usually in marsh or moorland. Frequents sewage farms, sand-dunes, tidal estuaries. Resident, generally distributed.

GREENSHANK

Description Larger than Redshank, with longer legs green, bill upturned. Upperparts grey; underparts white, with head, neck and sides of breast greyish, streaked darker. Length 12″.

Field Marks Like Redshank, has bobbing motion of head when feeding, often wading in shallow water. Also has a side-to-side motion of bill. Erratic, rapid flight. Loud " tchew tchew " note.

Nest and Distribution Nests on ground. Summer visitor, breeding on N. and W. Scottish moorlands, near lochs. Also visits salt marshes, estuaries, on migration.

GOLDEN PLOVER

Description Mottled black and gold upperparts, face and throat greyish, underparts black, speckled with white or with yellow. Lighter in winter. Underwing white, rump and tail darker in flight. Length 11″.

Field Marks Feeds on ground in parties, often with Lapwings, flies in compact flocks. Upright carriage, tilting whole body when feeding. Musical " tlui " note.

Nest and Distribution Nests on peaty ground in upland moors. Otherwise frequents arable land, grass fields, shores. Resident; generally distributed in winter; breeds chiefly in Scotland, Pennines, and Wales.

Description Very long bill, buff stripe down middle of head, longitudinal stripes on dark-brown upperparts.   Underparts white to buff, with dark-brown markings on neck and breast. Flanks barred. Length 10½″, bill 2½″.

Field Marks On rising zigzags rapidly, uttering hoarse note. Also flies in wide circles during breeding season, descending rapidly with " drumming " noise made by tail feathers. Prefers to feed in evening, spends day under cover.

Nest and Distribution Nests in grass clumps on ground, usually near bog. Resident, generally distributed. Favours marshy moorlands, peaty hillsides, rushy fields.

SNOW BUNTING

Description Rather stocky build. Appears white in flight because of white underparts. Male has white underwing all seasons, black back and tail feathers, mottled brown in winter. Female and young greyish-brown upperparts, flecked black. Length 5½″.

Field Marks Nearly always on ground in small parties. Undulating flight, skims before settling. Musical " tirr-ip " song.

 **Nest and Distribution** Nests among loose boulders high up on mountain sides. Descends to rocky seashores in winter. Handful breed on highest Scottish mountains, but fairly widespread in winter.

REED BUNTING

Description Chestnut-brown upperparts, mottled with black; greyish to buff underparts. White outer-tail feathers. Male: black head and throat, white collar. Female and young: brown head, with buff eye stripe and throat, and dark moustachial streak. Length 6″.

Field Marks Tinkling " tweek tweek " song. Perches on reed stems or bushes, flicking wings and spreading tail. Jerky flight.

Nest and Distribution Nests in tussocks in marshy ground or reed beds. Visits cultivated fields in winter. Resident, generally distributed.

BIRDS OF THE SEA AND SHORE

KITTIWAKE

Description Smaller and more lightly built than most other gulls, the Kittiwake can also be distinguished by the black tips of its long, slender grey wings: it has no white at the tip, as do other gulls. The underparts are white, but the young bird has a black yoke across its neck. The mantle is lavender grey, legs are black-brown. Beak yellow. Length 16″.

Field Marks Kittiwake has the wildest and most buoyant flight of all the gulls. It follows vessels far out to sea, and is not often seen near the shore. At nesting time, its harsh " kittiwaak " call can be heard on suitable headlands and islands.

Nest and Distribution Unlike many gulls, who lay their eggs on the bare rock, Kittiwakes construct a well-shaped nest of grass and other materials, and nest in large colonies on ledges of cliffs, and in gullies and caves. Resident; nests on all rocky coasts, especially the north and west.

GUILLEMOT

Description Upperparts are very dark brown, almost black. Underparts are white, and in winter throat and cheeks are also white. The bill is pointed. Some guillemots, especially in the north, have a white ring around the eye, with a white line running back from it over the side of the head. Length 16″.

Field Marks They spend most of the time swimming and diving in off-shore waters, seldom coming inland or to coastal waters except to nest. At this time the harsh cawing of thousands of birds may be heard as they gather on steep cliff faces. The parent bird dives for fish, brings up one at a time, the tail hanging from its beak. They fly a few feet above the waves with rapid whirring of their rather short wings. Upright carriage and black-and-white plumage resembles a penguin's.

Nest and Distribution Eggs are laid without a nest in large colonies on cliff ledges of rocky islands and wild coasts. Resident; breeds on all coasts except between Yorks and the Isle of Wight.

RAZOR-BILL

Description Thick, black bill has white line. Dark upperparts, with white wing-bar. Underparts white. Head and neck white, but black in breeding season except for white eye. Length 16″.

Field Marks Gregarious, travels in long formation low over water. Rides high on waves, with tail elevated.

Nest and Distribution Lays egg on cliff ledge or in crevice, also on rocky shores, in colonies. Resident: all suitable coasts except between Yorks and Isle of Wight.

BLACK-HEADED GULL

Description Conspicuous white margin at front edge of narrow black-tipped wings. Red bill and legs; yellowish in young. Head chocolate brown, but white, with dark markings, in winter. Underparts white, mantle grey, mottled brown in young. Length 13".

Field Marks Found inland and in cities as well as on shore. Said to trample on wet sand to bring up worms, and follows plough. Catches insects on wing, also plunges underwater.

Nest and Distribution Nests in colonies on ground near water or in marshy places, often inland. Resident, breeds locally throughout Britain.

TERN (COMMON)

Description Tern is a small, slender, graceful bird, with a long forked tail. The mantle is pale grey, the underparts white. Has a black cap and red, black-tipped bill. Legs are also red. Closely resembles Arctic Tern, which has an all-red bill. (Sandwich Tern—largest of the British terns—has a dark, yellow-tipped bill and dark legs.) Length 14″.

Field Marks Usually seen in flocks, skimming over sand-dunes and over the waves. The flight is buoyant, the body rising and falling with each wing beat. They seldom fly to a great height, as do other gulls. They dive for their fish, and are not scavengers. Their cry is a harsh strident " quee-arr ".

Nest and Distribution Terns nest in colonies, usually laying the eggs in a hollow in the sand-dunes; sand-spits and rocky islets are other favourite nesting-places. Summer visitor, breeding on all coasts.

HERRING GULL

Description Commonest gull on coast. Larger, heavier bird than Common Gull, with coarser bill, and pink, not greenish, legs and feet. Bill is yellow, with red spot. Mantle of adult is pale grey, with head and neck streaked brown in winter. Juveniles are mottled brown all over with mantle a darker brown. It takes three years for a bird to attain adult plumage. Underparts become white in adult. Wing-tips are black and white. Dark band on tail. Length 22″.

Field Marks Gregarious at all seasons. Tramples on sand, drops shells from height, catches insects in mid-air, and plunges underwater. Loud wailing cry.

Nest and Distribution Nests in colonies on cliff ledge or grassy slope. Keeps mainly to coasts and tidal estuaries, but often found on inland waters. Resident.

COMMON GULL

Description   Dark, blue-grey upperparts, white underparts, wings tipped with black and white. Greenish bill has no red spot. Legs greenish-yellow. Tapered outline when at rest given by wing-tips projecting beyond body. Juvenile mottled brown. Length 16″.

Field Marks   Drops shells from height, and plunges underwater. These and other habits, similar to other gulls. Cry, high-pitched " keee-ya ".

Nest and Distribution   Nests in small colonies on inland lakes and moorlands as well as on coast. Does not nest on cliffs. Resident; common breeder in Scottish Highlands and W. Ireland; otherwise widespread in winter.

BLACK-HEADED GULL

GREAT BLACK-BACKED GULL

Description Black mantle. Wings are tipped with white, and have white border all round. Tail white. Pink or whitish legs, yellow bill with red spot. Juvenile is mottled with brown, as other young gulls, but there is more contrast between mantle and underparts, which become white in adult. White head of adult bird is streaked grey in winter. Length 25–27".

Field Marks Less gregarious than most gulls, it is usually seen alone or in pairs, but sometimes in gatherings. Robs food from other gulls, sometimes catches smaller birds or even small animals such as lambs. Also eats fish, insects and garbage.

Nest and Distribution Nests on cliff ledges or rocky ground, not always in colonies. Found also on sandy coasts and islands. Infrequent inland. Resident; south and west coasts England, all coasts Wales and Scotland.

SHAG

Description Similar to Cormorant, but smaller, and more restricted habitat. Long-necked, aquatic bird, with slender bill and untidy crest. Plumage dark, oily green. Yellow around bill. Juvenile is brownish, sometimes white spot on chin. Length 30″.

Field Marks Flies low over water with neck extended. When diving, often springs up first. Perches on rocks, spreading wings to dry. Harsh croak.

Nest and Distribution Nests in colonies on ledges or among rocks. Restricted to rocky coasts. Resident, on west coasts.

CORMORANT

Description   Large, black-looking bird, with long, hooked bill. Plumage at close range is bronze-brown on upperparts, glossy green-blue on underparts.   In breeding season, head and neck have some grey feathers, and there is noticeable white patch on thigh, with white chin and cheeks, and base of bill yellow.   Young are brownish, with dull white breast.   Length 36".

Field Marks   Skilled fisher, diving again and again from same rock.   When alarmed, sinks whole body except for head and neck. Can dive noiselessly, but sometimes springs clear of water and plunges.   Perches on rocks, buoys, poles, with upright carriage and wings held out to dry.   Flies with neck extended, sometimes soars high.   Distinguished from divers, when on water, by tail and hooked bill, and head carried slightly uptilted.

Nest and Distribution   Nests in colonies on rocky islands or cliffs, occasionally inland in trees.   Resident, generally distributed on all coasts and some inland lakes in winter.

114

FULMAR PETREL

Description Rather like a gull, but distinguished by thicker neck, wings, and by flight. Wings, which are only slightly curved (not angled), are dark grey and not black-tipped. Plumage mostly white or yellowish-white, with grey mantle. The bill is very thick at tip. Length 18″.

Field Marks Flight distinct from that of gulls: long glides, with wings rigidly held, then leisurely flapping, very low over water. At breeding season, wheels to and fro beside cliff. Often has difficulty taking off. When alarmed, emits a spurt of oily liquid from mouth. Note, a guttural cackling, but often silent.

Nest and Distribution Nests in colonies on cliff. Mainly a deep-sea bird, but found on rocky coasts during summer months. St. Kilda has largest colony.

LONG-TAILED DUCK

Description Only male has long tail. Male has white head with dark cheeks; neck, wing patch and belly white; breast and middle of back brown. Female: whole back mottled brown, and all whites slightly dusky. Both have dark-brown wings. In summer, male is brown, with white cheeks and belly. Length 22″.

Field Marks Keeps well away from shore. Travels in flocks, gives clear, ringing call.

Nest and Distribution Winter visitor. Does not nest in Britain. Most frequent on east coasts of England and Scotland.

GANNET

Description   Distinctive cigar shape is given by pointed tail and long pointed beak. A large, white bird, with long, narrow, black-tipped wings. Juvenile is brownish all over, speckled with white, has same shape as adult. Length 36″; very large wing span.

Field Marks   Does a spectacular dive when fishing: drops with folded wings from a height, and plunges with great splash deep under-water. Regular, rapid wing beats, sometimes low over water, with occasional gliding and soaring. Usually silent, except near breeding places: loud, hoarse " urgh ".

Nest and Distribution   Breeds in large colonies on cliff ledge or on grassy slope above cliff. Frequents off-shore waters, never seen inland. Breeds on rocky islets off Scottish Western Isles, also Ireland and Wales (Grassholm).

117

RED-BREASTED MERGANSER

Description Male has chestnut breast which looks at a distance like a dark band. Belly is white, flanks mottled grey and white. Distinctive crest stands up on green head. Saw-edged bill is red, and there is white collar. Female and young duller, being brownish-grey, with whitish throat patch. Fore-wing is blackish, part nearer body is white with two black bands. Length 24″.

Field Marks Keeps off shore except at breeding season, frequently visiting bays and estuaries. Flies low over water, and swims moving neck backwards and forwards. Submerges most of back when alarmed. Dives after fish, feeding in shallows. Generally silent.

Nest and Distribution Nests on ground in hollow among boulders or tree roots. Resident in most of Scotland and parts of Ireland; winter visitor elsewhere. Breeds in vicinity of freshwater lakes and rivers as well as on coast.

STORM PETREL

Description This is the smallest of Petrels and the smallest web-footed bird. A sooty-black bird, with only rump white. Young resemble adults. Length 6″.

Field Marks Spends most of its time at sea, fluttering close to water with almost unceasing wing beats, often pattering on waves or floating buoyantly. Frequently follows vessels. Never occurs inland, unless storm-driven, and goes ashore only to breed, when it feeds its young at night, leaving nest during the day to go back to sea. Silent, except on nest, when it has penetrating " urr chick " note. When alarmed will eject oily spurt from mouth.

Nest and Distribution Nests in colonies among loose boulders or in burrow. Resident in Scilly Isles, S.W. coast of England, Wales, Ireland, and Scottish isles.

GOOSANDER

Description Largest of " sawbills ". In shape, resembles Red-Breasted Merganser, but is much larger. In flight, the male looks strikingly black and white. Underparts are white, tinged with pink, and head is dark green. The back is black. Female has back and flanks grey, and white underparts, with head chestnut, except for mane-like crest. Juveniles resemble female, but are duller, with shorter crest; both have white patch on chin. Length 26″.

Field Marks Swims low in the water, submerging whole back when alarmed, and diving and swimming underwater when fishing. Rises with difficulty and flies low over water, following bend of streams. Perches on rocks, trees, or on shore. Generally silent.

Nest and Distribution Nests in tree hollows, sometimes in boulders or among heather, near river or lake. Frequents fairly wooded lake country, and some sea inlets. Resident, mainly N. Scotland; winter visitor farther south.

PUFFIN

Description Black-and-white plumage, bright red feet, and remarkable bill make this bird easy to recognize. Bill has triangular, rather parrot-like shape, and is very large and brightly coloured. The juvenile bird has a smaller, more normally shaped bill, and the female has more yellow feet. Length 12″.

Field Marks Usually stands upright, and is generally seen in large flocks. Flies in small arc, with very quick beats of its short wings. Has only one note, a low " arr, arr ". Dives after fish, returning to the surface with several fish hanging from the beak.

Nest and Distribution Nests in burrows, occasionally in crevice or under boulder, in large colonies on grassy cliff-tops. Frequents off-shore waters, usually only a short distance from land. Resident, breeding at suitable sites on south and west coasts of England and Wales, Scottish isles, and Ireland.

SHEARWATER

Description Black above, white below; flies so that these two colours are alternately displayed. Bill hooked at tip. Long narrow wings. Length 14″.

Field Marks Flight distinctive: glides on rigid wings, tilting over now on one side, now the other, so that wing seems to touch water. Large flocks assemble just off shore at sunset during breeding season. Otherwise keeps to open sea, but does not follow ships.

Nest and Distribution Nests in colonies in burrows. Summer visitor to Scilly and other western isles.

COMMON SCOTER

Description The male is the only black wild duck in Britain (except Velvet Scoter, which has white wing-bar): the plumage is sooty black all over, only relief being orange patch on black bill, and bluish bulb at base of bill. Female is dark brown, with paler shade at sides of head, and legs more brown than black. Length 20″.

Field Marks Rides buoyantly on waves, sinking body, except for head, when alarmed. Dives after shellfish, especially mussels. Rises with difficulty, and flies low over water, or sometimes quite high, in flocks. Formation varies from irregular line to wedge-shape. Rarely seen inland, but sometimes rests on sandbanks. Plaintive piping call and " tuk tuk " note are male's. Female's note is hoarser.

Nest and Distribution Nests in heather close to water of highland loch, or on wooded island (especially in Ireland). Outside breeding season keeps to open sea not too far off shore. Resident. Breeds N. Scotland, Ireland, W. Scottish islands. Also winter visitor on some other coasts.

OYSTER CATCHER

Description An unmistakable bird, with smart black-and-white plumage, long orange bill, and long pink legs. Head, breast and back are glossy black. Underparts and wing-bar, white. Juvenile has all parts mottled brown. Length 17″.

Field Marks Usually seen in flocks. Walks sedately on seashores and mud-flats, looking for food, mussels, limpets, worms; or runs rapidly. Noisy and excitable and often active far into the night. Flies low over water and sometimes settles thereon. The call note is a loud " kleep kleep ".

Nest and Distribution The nest is a hollow on the ground on the sea-shore, sand-dunes, or in Scotland, on rivers and lochs. Resident; fairly common on all coasts, especially as winter visitor.

128

Cuculus canorus 13 in.

No sound in nature is awaited more eagerly in these islands than the loud, ringing, repeated song of the cuckoo. The male's song, with its promise that summer is not far off, is a national institution, important enough in Britain's country calendar to be dignified by letters to *The Times*. The first cuckoos of the year usually arrive in the second or third week of April from their winter quarters in Africa. March cuckoos are not unknown, but more often than not these early birds turn out to be schoolboys, hoaxing over-eager listeners.

When it is seen on the wing, a cuckoo can easily be mistaken for a male sparrowhawk. But it can be identified by its heavier appearance, pointed wings, and long, graduated tail, spotted and tipped with white.

After their arrival, cuckoos spread out over almost the whole of the British Isles into any kind of country where they can find foster-parents for their young. The double-noted 'cuckoo', heard over woods and thickets, heaths, sand-dunes, moorland and hills, is the male's courtship song. The female has a bubbling trill.

When mating is over, the adult birds leave Britain, flying south in July and early August. The newly fledged young linger until September after leaving their foster-parents. Then they migrate, finding their way unaided to their winter quarters—a remarkable example of a bird's inborn ability to navigate.

IDENTIFICATION *grey head and back, barred underparts; distinguished from sparrowhawk by slender bill, pointed wings and graduated, spotted tail; song distinctive; sexes alike, though a rare variety occurs in which female is chestnut-coloured and barred above and below; juveniles are brown and barred with white spots on the head.*

TURNSTONE

Description Strikingly pied in flight. Head and throat black and white, rump white, mottled chestnut and black mantle, black band across breast. Short orange legs. Female and young duller. Both sexes darker in winter. Length 9″.

Field Marks Seen in small parties on rocky beaches, where it turns over stones and weeds. Flight slow and wavering, but can fly swiftly and strongly. Note, a metallic chatter.

Nest and Distribution Does not breed in Britain. Found on all coasts, very rare inland.

BRENT GOOSE

Description The smallest and darkest of the geese. Head, neck and upper breast are black, and upperparts are dark grey-brown. There is a white patch on the side of neck of adult birds. The under-tail coverts are white, shading to greyish-white or grey on the breast. The tail quills are black, as are the feet and bill. Length 22″.

Field Marks Gregarious, it is sometimes found in huge flocks, flying in irregular formation not too far from ground. Flight is swift but rather heavy. The white under-tail parts are conspicuous. Note is a single, guttural " krrowk ". Comes ashore only to feed.

Nest and Distribution A winter visitor, the Brent Goose does not breed in Britain. It occurs in large flocks on tidal flats and estuaries of E. and S. England. In Scotland it occurs on east and west coasts.

SHELD DUCK

Description A large, boldly patterned bird, more like a goose than a duck. At a distance appears to be black and white, but at close quarters gay plumage can be seen. Head and neck are glossy black with metallic green lights. Shoulders and underparts are white, with broad chestnut band around middle, and a greyish band down centre. Wings are white, bordered with black, and white tail is also black-edged. Bill is bright red and the drake has a red knob at the base. Juvenile duller. Length 25″.

Field Marks Occurs in large flocks, wading in shallow water or resting on shore. Flight is swift and easy. Often rests on the sea, but keeps near shore.

Nest and Distribution Nests in burrow or under rocks and bushes, usually on rough ground on cliff-tops, or near lakes, and occasionally inland. Otherwise keeps to sandy or muddy coasts or estuaries. Resident, generally distributed on suitable coasts.

DUNLIN

Description   The commonest of shore birds.   Characteristics are round-shouldered pose, long straight bill, greyish-brown plumage, with black patch on lower breast in summer.   White wing-bar conspicuous.   Length 7¼".

Field Marks   Feeds along tide line in large numbers.   Flocks sweep over sea or flats, tilting so that alternate light and dark plumage is seen.

Nest and Distribution   Nests on ground close to water.   Resident; frequents muddy shores, estuaries, and salt marshes.   Generally distributed, breeds W. and N. Britain, on inland moors.

HERON

Description One of the largest of British birds. Long bill and legs, and grey, white and black plumage make it easy to recognize. Upperparts and tail are grey, head and long slender neck white, with black eye streak, and black and blue streaks on front of neck. Underparts greyish-white. Wing is black-bordered. Length 36″.

Field Marks Flies with long neck either extended, or neatly tucked between shoulders. Wing beats are slow and regular, and legs are extended behind like streamers. On the ground most of the time, it has slow, deliberate walk, often stands motionless on one leg. Sometimes perches on trees. Wades in shallow water, with neck curved ready to catch fish. Gregarious. Has loud raucous voice.

Nest and Distribution Large nests are found high in trees, in colonies. Resident; generally distributed, especially in S.E. England and Scotland. Found in any watery place.

ARCTIC SKUA

Description One of the largest and fiercest of the gulls. Distinguished by dark plumage and two long feathers which project beyond the rest of the tail. Most Arctic Skuas are uniform dark brown, with paler neck and sides of face, but many have pale, yellowish-tinged underparts and neck, with the head appearing as a black cap. Length 20″.

Field Marks Swift and graceful flight, with hawk-like gliding and leisurely flapping. Hawk-like in habits also, it preys on smaller birds, stealing the food which they are carrying or the eggs in their nests. Also feeds on small mammals. Has wailing, mewing voice.

Nest and Distribution Nests in colonies on turfy cliff-tops or moorland. Otherwise a marine bird. Summer visitor. Breeds in N. Scottish isles, but is seen as passage migrant on all coasts.

BARNACLE GOOSE

Description Boldly patterned in black, white and grey. Crown, neck and breast glossy black, face and forehead white, upperparts bluish-grey, barred with black and narrow strips of white. Short bill. Black tail and legs. Length 25″.

Field Marks Flies in flocks, has barking call. Feeds mostly at night, on sand-dunes, or grasslands near shore, sometimes mud-flats. Rests on the sea, never found far inland.

Nest and Distribution Winter visitor, mostly to Hebrides, but also other coasts.

138

PURPLE SANDPIPER

Description Rather stocky little bird, with short, yellowish legs. Dark-brown back has purplish lights at close range. Variegated effect is given by pale edgings to feathers. Throat whitish, flanks white with prominent dark markings. Underparts grey. White wing-bar conspicuous in flight. Length 8".

Field Marks Keeps mostly to rocks on shores, where it looks for food. Swims readily, flies only occasionally, low over water. Found in small parties.

Nest and Distribution Winter visitor to all coasts, especially rocky ones. Hardly ever seen inland.

RINGED PLOVER

Description Sturdily built, with prominent black collar, bold black-and-white markings on side and front of head, and white wing-bar, conspicuous in flight. Underparts white. Back and crown brown. Tail brown, with white edging. Legs orange-yellow. Juvenile duller. Length 7¾″.

Field Marks Runs rapidly with head up, tilts whole body when feeding. Bobs head nervously. Crouching carriage when leaving nest. Flight is rapid, low. Trilling song.

Nest and Distribution Nests on sand, turf, shingle. Resident, generally distributed on sandy or muddy shores.

GOLDEN-EYE

Description Bold black-and-white pattern of drake distinctive even at long range. He has black head with green and purple gloss, and distinctive circular white patch between eye and bill. Back and tail are black; neck, underparts and sides are white; black streaks on shoulders and flanks. Wings black, with conspicuous white patch on lower half. Short bill and peaked crown give triangular outline. Female and young have same distinctive outline, and the white wing patch, but are chocolate-headed, and mottled grey. Length 19".

Field Marks Rapid wing beats make characteristic loud singing sound. Rises easily from water. Puffs out neck feathers when excited. Found in small parties. Dives underwater.

Nest and Distribution Winter visitor, frequenting sea coasts, tidal estuaries, river mouths, and inland waters. In Scotland it is also seen in summer, but does not breed.

INDEX

SEDGE WARBLER
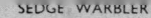

BLACKCAP

ROBIN

RING OUZEL

GREAT BLACK-BACKED GULL

STARLING

CARRION CROW
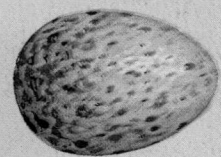

SANDWICH TERN

HERON
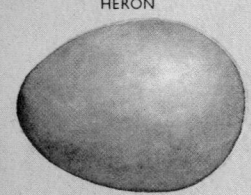

GOLDEN EAGLE
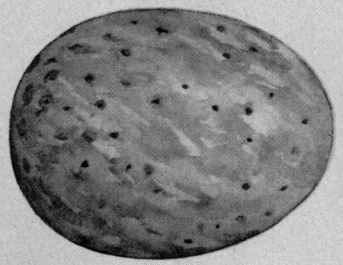

HERRING GULL
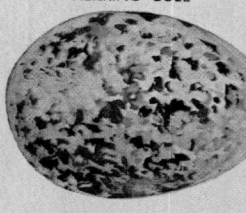

PARTRIDGE

MERLIN
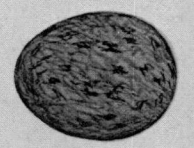

MAGPIE
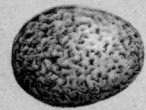

OYSTER CATCHER
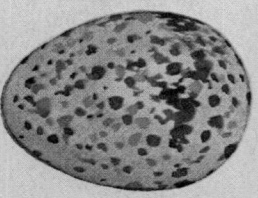

JACKDAW

SONG THRUSH

NIGHTINGALE

BLACKBIRD